OTHER BOOKS BY ROBERT M. DRAKE

Spaceship (2012)
The Great Artist (2012)
Science (2013)
Beautiful Chaos (2014)
Beautiful Chaos 2 (2014)
Black Butterfly (2015)
A Brilliant Madness (2015)
Beautiful and Damned (2016)
Broken Flowers (2016)
Gravity: A Novel (2017)
Star Theory (2017)
Chaos Theory (2017)
Light Theory (2017)
Moon Theory (2017)
Dead Pop Art (2017)
Chasing The Gloom: A Novel (2017)
Moon Matrix (2018)
Seeds of Wrath (2018)
Dawn of Mayhem (2018)
The King is Dead (2018)
What I Feel When I Don't Want To Feel (2019)
What I Say To Myself When I Need To Calm The
Fuck Down (2019)
What I Say When I'm Not Saying A Damn Thing
(2019)
What I Mean When I Say Miss You, Love You &
Fuck You (2019)

For Excerpts and Updates please follow:

Instagram.com/rmdrk
Facebook.com/rmdrk
Twitter.com/rmdrk

ISBN: 978-1-7326901-0-3

Book Cover: Robert M. Drake

I'm In My Feelings Series

For The Ones Who Feel lost

CONTENTS

What I Say When I'm Not Saying A Damn Thing

ROBERT M. DRAKE

WHAT IS IT

What is it that you're avoiding?
Is it love?
Is it friendship?

I know you're exhausted.
I can see it in your eyes.

I know you've been through hell.

I know your heart is worn
and beaten.

I know.

You don't have to say a word.

I sense it.

I can feel what hurts.
I can relate to your pain.

To your tragedy.

You're sad,
of course you are...

Because you think
your life isn't going as planned.

Because almost everything
you do

leads you toward some kind
of terrible disappointment—

toward the wrong kind
of people to love.

It's hard.

All of it is.

From what you feel
to how you want to express yourself

and execute your heart
to the world.

It's hard
and letting others know
who you are is hard,

too hard.

I know,
but please...

Don't close your heart.

Don't walk away
from the possibility
and please don't stop believing.

Hope is a beautiful thing.

A miraculous thing
and everything you're going through
I feel as well.

Because you're not alone,
you never were

and you never will be.

So stop telling yourself
that you are.

Stop letting your mind
play tricks on you

and stop trying to convince yourself
that you are not capable
of love.

That you're not capable
of more—of what you deserve.

You're beautiful,
baby,

don't let your doubts destroy
who you really are.

Keep shining.

SOME, NOT ALL

Some good-byes
are easy
and then there are some
that are hard.

No one ever likes
letting people go.

No one ever likes
being the one
who cuts the line.

But what is right is right.

And you can't be with someone
if they love someone else.

You can't be with someone
because they're bored

or because
they're using you
to pass their time.

You can't.

That's not right.
That's not fair.

Find someone
who loves you
genuinely.

Find someone
who has grown from their past,

not someone who is *still*
living in it.

Find someone,
anyone, who'll make you
a better person.

That's the goal.

That's the reason we search

for certain people—for someone

to love…
and to hold.

HAVE NOT LEARNED

If life has taught us anything,
then it has taught us

that finding someone
you connect with

is just as rare
and as beautiful

as losing someone
you once loved

or cared about.

Life teaches us many things
but finding balance in receiving

and letting go
is just as important...

as finding balance
in happiness and sadness—in love

and pain.

Balance is key.

And sometimes you're going to win...

while other times

you're going to sit back
and cry.

And it's the same with people.

You lose one to gain another
and somewhere in-between
you must find peace.

You must accept the way
they come and go…

and understand

how they come to you
when you need them the most
and vice versa.

Life,
like people,

change

but the trick is
to remember those

who are worth remembering

and find balance

in all things

that are meant
to make you fall.

That are meant
to make you feel…

free.

LESS ALONE PT 3

You make me feel less alone
and I don't mean a time

or a place
or being together,

somewhere on the edge
of the world.

I mean,
when I'm alone in my bed.

Alone in the middle of the street.

Alone somewhere,
anywhere, on the planet.

When I close my eyes
or when I wake…

you make me *feel less alone.*

Because we're lovers,
you and I,

we look at the details
and let our hearts lead the way.

So whether we're together in a room
or cities apart,

or even countries,

I look up toward the moon
and feel secure.

And I do so
because

I know you're out there,
breathing...

surviving…

thinking and feeling
the same way as me.

And because of that...
I feel less alone.

I feel like you.

Like you and I are the last people
on the planet…

and we have our entire lives
to convince each other

and ourselves
of why we are capable of love—
of so much more.

We deserve it,

you and I,

we deserve people
who make us feel

less alone.

People who bring out
the best parts of eachother.

People who make us feel

like we are

in love
with ourselves.

YOU DON'T KNOW

You don't know
how hard it is

for me
to be myself.

For me to speak my mind
in a place

that keeps telling me
what to feel.

In a world that keeps
shoving me
with what to think.

So I say it like this

because

it is the only way
I know how.

These are my feelings:
black and white.

These are my scars:
hot and cold.

And you can either
accept them
or leave them.

Love them
or misunderstand them

for what they are.

This is what I do
and this is what I've done

and these are my
contradictions.

My flesh
is of my flesh

and my blood
is of my blood.

And I don't need
some asshole in the media

to tell me the difference
between the two.

Thisis my heart.
This is my mind.

And what connects the two

is a bridge
that only I can cross.

That only I can build
if it falls.

This is what hurts.
This is how my heart falls

and this is how
I heal the two,

bond the two.

And I will live
the way I must,

although,
the world will continue
to bring me pain.

Let me be
who I want to be

and let my mind travel
the undiscovered road
that waits ahead.

Let me allow
who I want
in my life.

And let me love freely
without conviction.

This is all I ask of you.
Is it too much?

You already have control
of everything else.

Let me have
a piece of myself back.

That is all I ask.

Let me love
who I want to love.

And let me do so
freely.

Give me a piece
of the world

and I will return it
back to you

better than it was
before.

IN SAND

It's not you.

It's just
you keep giving your heart

to the wrong
type of people.

People who haven't grown
or matured.

People who haven't
been through enough.

Who haven't been hurt
enough

to understand what it's like
to drown in sand—

what it's like to drown
in an ocean of fire.

So it's not you,
although,

they'll make you *think* it is
but it's not.

Believe me it's not.

It's just some people
have a way of pulling your heart.

Some people
have a way

of bringing out
different sides of you.

Both beautiful and ugly.

So it's definitely not your fault
for feeling too deeply.

For giving chances
and letting things in

the way you do.

And it's not your fault
for not knowing

what's good for you either.

Because it's hard
figuring things out like that.

It's hard
knowing what you deserve

and don't.

It's hard
choosing between

what's right for you
and what hurts,

no matter how much love
you have for those

who've done you wrong.

It's hard
and it takes time,

and there's no easy way to put it
without making you feel

some sort of way

but you have to *move on.*

You have to come
to the realization that some people

aren't meant
to be yours—no matter how much

history you have together
and no matter how much

time you've put into them.

You have to let go sometimes
and understand

that maybe it's not you
because you've done

all that you can.

That maybe it's them
and that maybe

starting over

can be the change you need

to move on...
after all.

GO SILENT

Don't tell them it's okay
when you know it's not.

Don't let your feelings fade
into the darkness.

Don't let your voice go silent.

Let them know
what's in your heart.

Let them know
how beautiful it is

to be understood.

How beautiful it is
to have someone you can trust—

to speak to
about anything.

Be open.

Share what's on your mind.

And never go quietly
into the dark.

People will always
appreciate you for your honesty,

and love you
for what you carry within your heart.

So speak up,
tell it how it is.

If it hurts,
then it hurts.

I just want to make sure
you're not censoring yourself.

You deserve so much more
than that,

and believe…

that the reassurance of self

is more valuable
than anything else.

EXCEPT HOPE

It is my will
to choose someone

who supports my appetite
for life.

Someone
who compels my voice.

Who strengthens my vision.

It is my will
to be with someone

who understands me.

Who makes me feel
real.

Someone who isn't afraid
to explore the soul—

the deeper meaning
of pain and love.

It is my will
to feed off their fire.

To live by it.

To exchange it
when needed most.

And to comfort each other
when things seem

to be falling apart.

It is my will,
and mine only...

and it should be yours
as well.

Life is too short
to not live it

any other way.

To not to chase
what you desire

or what you know
you deserve.

Life is too fragile
to *NOT* seek others

who seek the same things

and others who are looking
for another way out.

Another way to love.

To die.
To live.

To forgive and heal.

Find them,
for they are out there

and find them
because they are out

looking for you.

It is your will
and nothing is ever determined

except for hope.

Hope you find them

and

hope they are everything
you need

and more.

HOW MANY TIMES

You've got to ask yourself

how many times
can the same person break you.

How many times
can the same person
let you down.

And how many times
can you heal

without having some kind
of mental break down.

There must come a time
when you come to your senses.

A moment
where everything just connects,

when you realize
your value, your worth.

So you've got to ask yourself
these types of things.

Is it worth being unloved?

Is it worth being mistreated?

You know what you deserve
and deep down inside

something is telling you
to go, to move on,

but you're letting this pain,
this treatment,

go on
over and over again.

And it keeps cycling.

You cry.
You heal.
You make-up to break-up

with no end.

But how many times
can the same person destroy you?

Really, ask yourself this
and *question* this question.

Ask yourself when it is enough.
And if your answer
is hard to commit to,

then you must
re-evaluate everything,
question everything,

take time on yourself
and rediscover what you deserve.

Because no one
should be breaking you

without some kind of consequence.

No one should be tampering
with your heart

and what you feel.

No one should have that kind
of power over you.

You were born to live,
love, and learn,

and not have to go through
the same heart break

more than once.

Amen.

WHEN IT IS OVER

Sometimes when it's over...
it's over.

And what's worse about that

is,

how the person you thought
you'd spend the rest of your life

with vanishes.

They never return to you.

They just stay
in the back of your heart...

in limbo...

forever.

HARD TO TRUST

It's hard to trust people
when they tell you

they love you
but end up

breaking your heart.

It's hard to see people
for who they are

when they're really good
at keeping

their mask on.

REFLECTING WATER

Self-love isn't entirely
what we've been told.

It's not just about going
out for a run,

or rewarding yourself
with a new pair of shoes,

or even having
some alone time.

It's about accepting your past
and learning from your mistakes.

It's about reflecting
from within

and seeing yourself
for who you are.

It's about thinking twice
when presented with a difficult

situation.

It's about respecting others
and treating them as equals.

It's about owning up
to your actions

and moving forward,

regardless

of what your past
has shown you.

Self-love isn't just about you...

it's about you
and everyone around you.

It's about inspiring people
to do better.

And about encouraging
them to love themselves

and do the same.

MAKE SOMEONE CARE

You can't make someone care.

No matter how much love
you have for them.

Some people
will never understand

what it is
you do for them.

What it is
you feel for them.

And sadly,
most of them

will never realize your worth,
not until *you're gone.*

Not until
it's too late.

That's life.

Some people will let you down
and never will you forget
how they made you feel.

Some people
will break your heart

and never
will you have the opportunity
to see it coming.

And some people
will forever stay in your heart

and never
will you be able

to explain

why.

CLOUDS

The sad truth is,

it will never work
if you ignore them

when you're mad
or if you stay silent

when something
is eating you alive.

Whatever you do in life...
use your voice.

Tell people how you feel...
express yourself freely

and always
reflect what's in your heart.

There's no better way to live,
to understand,

and above all,
to love.

MONSTERS

No matter how terrible
someone has hurt you,

don't let them
turn you cruel.

Don't let them
turn your heart cold.

Someone out there
was born to love you

and they shouldn't suffer
because of the carelessness

of other people.

Forgive but don't forget.

Love and learn.
Let go and move on.

Not everyone is the same.

Not everyone will hurt you
the way they did.

There are still a few good ones

out there.

Trust the process.

There is always
a ray of light

somewhere
in the darkness...

waiting to be found.

THINK BEFORE

You've got to think
before you speak

sometimes.

You can't just tell someone
you hate them

and love them
the next.

You can't just
say something hurts

just because you're mad.

Things happen.

People are going to
do things

to disappoint you.

They're going to piss you off.

That's how it is,
you know.

That's how people work.

No one gets along
all the time.

No one is perfect,
you know?

So you should learn
to hold your tongue
a little tighter.

Bring it in a little—
reflect a little,

you know.

Not everything
is meant to destroy you

but sometimes
words

can destroy another person,
and the wrong ones

can cause them
to go mad.

Because words hurt
far more than swords.

Than bombs.
Than anything else.

They can burn through the soul.

Break the mind
and heart in ways we can't imagine.

And there's nothing scarier
than that.

Than causing some kind
of terrible harm

without anything
but the use of words.

So please,
speak kindly when you're mad.

Take a step back
when you're broken.

And don't lash out
at everyone you see.

Some people genuinely care,
therefore,

we shouldn't let trivial things
get in the way.

Words kill
and sometimes

there's no coming back

from that type
of crucifixion

at all.

ELSE FAILS

Let me love you
when all else fails.

Let me be there for you.

Let me show you
how there are still some good
people out there.

Let me help you
get over whatever it is
that's hurting you.

Let me love you
the way you need to

be loved.

Let me,
you won't regret it

and neither would I.

I want to love you.
I want to be that one person

you depend on
when you're feeling blue.

That one person
you need

when the world starts falling down.

Let me love you

because we both know
we have everything to gain

and yet,
nothing to lose.

HALF EMPTY

Just because you care for them
doesn't give them

the right to hurt you.

It doesn't give them
the right
to only reach you

when they need something
from you.

You need to realize
who is who

and realize
that maybe you're loving

the wrong kind
of people.

Because you shouldn't feel
half empty, half full.

You shouldn't be questioning
their actions

and yours either.

That's not love.
That's not friendship.

That's not how it works.

I'm sorry to say
that maybe you've spent

too much time
chasing the wrong people.

That maybe
you've miscalculated
what you deserve.

I'm sorry to say
that maybe it's time
to move on.

Time to let go.
Time to heal

but also
time to grow.

It's time,
of course it is.

Time for you
to spend all of that love
on yourself.

Time for you
to re-spark

what it is
that matters to you.

And it's going to be hard
because nothing is ever easy.

But like I said,
just because you care,

it doesn't give them the right
to hurt you.

And ironically,
you could still care

but just make sure
it's well spent

on other people—on people
who feel the same way

you feel.

What I'm trying to say is,
you shouldn't exhaust the star within you

on people
who are far too afraid

to appreciate
its light.

Stay beautiful,
my friends.

YOU ARE WORTH IT

Your worth
is not determined

by the amount of people
who love you.

Your worth
is immeasurable,
as it should be.

No one can claim it.

No one can tell you
how much you should love
or not love.

There is no scale.
No form.

No definition
or fashion

that could determine it,
define it.

Your value—your worth,
is based on how you weigh yourself,

on how you love
yourself
and take care
of yourself.

And it will never be determined
by another person.

So you could have
a million people

who love you,
but none of it is going to matter

if you don't love yourself.
If you don't

care about your future
or worry about the way you feel.

This I tell
to all the people I love:

"Love yourself.
I cannot stress it enough.

And I don't mean
buying yourself something.

I don't mean
taking an extra hour

of sleep, etc.

I mean,
love yourself.

Respect yourself.
Forgive yourself.

It's okay to make a mistake.
It's okay to get your heart broken.

To care more
than you should.

It's okay to fall
a hundred times.

It's okay...
all of it is...

as long as you take
something from it

and learn
about yourself— about

who you are
and what you can handle."

This I tell
to the people I love:

"Self-love
is worth a thousand words

but none will matter
if they are not defined

or shaped
or valued
or held
or loved

by no one...

other than you."

CATCH MYSELF

And I'm wondering
how many people you've met

since I've been gone.

And how many of them
you've fallen in love with

and how many of them
you've changed.

And I'm wondering
if you've had your heart broken

and if you've learned
to move on—if you've learned

to let go of the past.

I'm thinking about you, kid,
and I'm sorry

about how careless
I was.

It's just
back then,

I didn't know
what I was doing.

I didn't know
how to tell you

how it was—how much
you meant to me.

And now,
after all this time,

I catch myself thinking about you,
wondering what has become

of your life.

It's sad.

And I don't expect you
to feel the same way

because I know
how different it must be

for you.

But nonetheless,
around here,

it's never been the same

without you,
and sadly,

I can't remember
what it was like before you.

Sometimes,
when I'm alone,

the moments we once had
haunt me

and they remind me
of how wrong I was

for letting you go.

Sometimes,
when I'm alone,

the darkness becomes darker
than before

and sometimes
the only thing that keeps me going

is the memory
of what we once had.

Because I really hurt you
and I regret it,

and I do so,
so fiercely—deeply.

But the hours keep accumulating
and the calendars keep piling

in the trash
and the rooms in my heart
remain empty.

And like all good things that pass...
it is far too late

to bring you back home.

Far too late
to pick up the phone

to tell you...
how much I still care.

I'm sorry, kid...

wherever you are,
I hope you're doing well.

I hope you're living out your dream
and I hope

you've outgrown what hurts.
Stay young, my love,

and stay…
forever free.

THE PAUSE

And like all things
that hurt,

like all things
that are meant

to change your life,

the moment you discover
who it is you love...

what it is you love...
it vanishes

in an instant
before your naked eyes.

I'm sorry to say this,

but

there's no other way to put it.

Nothing is forever.
Nothing last long enough
to claim it as your own.

Nothing,

no matter how much
you put into it,

get out of it.

Nothing is ever yours
to keep.

You must learn
to free yourself of attachment

but you must also
learn to appreciate things,

people,
places,
and moments.

You must learn to love them
for what they are.

Learn to hold on
when you must

and let go
when there's no other way.

You must learn many things
as I have

and once you do,

you will discover
how not much can harm you

besides what you let in.

You must learn this,
there's no other way.

I'm sorry to sound so dark.

It's just...
that's the way I see it.

That's all.

The goal isn't to live
with the fear of loss,

disappointment,
and despair.

The goal is to understand
all these things

and accept them
for what they are.

BOTH WAYS

It works both ways.

Sometimes you're going to hurt
someone you love,

someone you care about.

Sometimes you're going to
mistreat them

and for a moment
forget how important
they are to you.

Sometimes you're going to wish
you never met them,

you're going to wish
them gone.

And sometimes...

they'll do the exact same things to you.

While other times,
they won't.

This way of life

should be simple.

You should love
the ones you love

and try to never disappoint them.

And love
the ones who've never felt
love
even harder.

You get
what you put out.

You get
what you deserve.

The universe works
in mysterious ways

and almost always
does it bring you both

love and loss.

Both the people you need
and the people you don't.

Almost always,
does it bring you these things

when you need them most.

But never,
ever…

does it bring them to you
at the same time.

THE FLOWERS DOOM

Forget the flowers.
Forget the cards.

Give her…
her soul back,
her voice back.

Give her
everything the world took

and let her be
who she wants to be.

Let her feel
what she wants to feel.

Let her deal
with her problems
and her own life

her way.

She doesn't want
to be saved.

She doesn't want
to be guided toward the right direction.

Let her have
her own mistakes.

Her own lessons,
her own heartbreaks.

And let her solve them
on her own.

She doesn't need someone...

What she needs is
for everyone to leave her

the fuck alone

and let her live
her life

as she wants to.

That's all.

NOT SO BAD

I don't want to begin
with the bad things

because from here on out
you should only focus

on the good,
therefore,

and I say this
with my soul…

the *good thing* is,
you can always start over.

So don't let
the bad stuff discourage you
from meeting someone new.

Just take the time you need
to heal, to make peace

with your past,
and take all the time you need

to do so.

No one is going to force you

into anything.

No one is going to
question what you decide
to do either.

The world is your oyster
and you have the right

to start over
as many times

as you want,
as long as it makes you

happy.

As long as it
stands for something

and as long as it
brings you closer

to all the things
you deserve

to feel.

FLAWS

And with all her flaws,
she has performed

somewhat
of a miracle.

She has saved me
from myself.

She has saved me
from terrible anguish.

From all the fires
many have died from.

From all demons
and the darkness that consumes
the human heart.

She has made me realize
how sometimes,

*all it takes
is one person*

*to free you
from yourself.*

THE ANSWER

You see,
that's the problem.

You think
there's always tomorrow.

You think
you'll always have
another chance,

another day.

You think
you'll always have enough time
to say the things

you feel.

Enough time to spend
with those you love the most.

And then,
one day,

out of the blue,
that day arrives.

The day you thought

would never come.

You wake up in a place
where you no longer have

the opportunity

to say the things
you've wanted to say.

To spend the time with those
who mattered most.

The truth becomes rain

and it pours
and it floods

and you might drown
in the chaos of regret...

it has no mercy
on your soul.

Do not become this person.

Do not kill yourself
over the "what if"...

over the "how come"
and "why."

Do not let the opportunity
slip through your hands.

Do not take the moment
for granted.

There is nothing glorious
in dwelling over what should've

been done or said.

There's nothing holy
in overthinking...

in losing yourself
within the lost possibility.

There is no other moment
more beautiful than this one,

and there is no other way to live.

You should always say
what you feel

and never take the people you love
for granted...

Otherwise,
once they're gone,
they're gone.

And what's left undone
will haunt you...

forever.

It will follow you to the grave,
keep you company

and remind you
of how badly

you let
things go.

WHAT YOU DO

Whatever you do,

do not fall
into the nothingness.

Do not fall
into the lies.

If you must fill the void,
then by all means...

let it be filled
with something real.

With something
that matters

and with something
you cannot live without.

No matter how isolated
you feel.

ALL IS EMPTY

No matter how empty
your heart feels,

you have to believe
that everyone you meet

is sent to you
when you need them most.

So whether you're laughing
or crying...

believe

how it is all connected.

Believe

how there is no other way
to get through the chapters

of your life.

From the moment you meet
to the moment they're gone.

People come into your life
because they must

and exit
when there's nothing left
for you to receive…

when the experience
and lesson have been fulfilled

and learned.

It's a blessing and a curse,
of course it is.

You love,
to lose,
and lose,

to rediscover the *love again.*

And each time
it is different

but almost always,
does it end…

the same.

DO NOT SPEAK

Do not tell me I am empty.

That I have no soul.
That your eyes

pierce through mine
and make you feel
nothing.

Don't tell me I do not care.

That your expectation of me
was not fulfilling enough.

Do not tell me who I am,

or rather,
who you think I am.

I do not want to hear it.
I do not want to give in to it.

I have been through hell
or at least,

I think I have.

I have been through enough

or at least,
enough to make me feel

as if I do not need
to express myself as you desire,

give myself
how you want me to.

I cannot read your mind.

I cannot do the things
you would like me to do.

I have my own mind.

My own heart.
My own darkness
and my own light.

And sometimes,
I carry them on my hands,

in plain sight,
for people like you to see.

And most of the time,
they go unnoticed.

My weep goes silent.
My heart breaks

without making a sound.

But I'm not falling apart
over it.

I know how strong I am.
I know what I have been through

and I understand
how much more I have to endure.

So yes,
I do love you.

I do care.
I do think about you

when you are not around.

I just do not know
how to show it

without making
a part of you cry.

Without making
a part of you angry.

And without making
a part of you

believe

that I am not the one
for you.

I want to love you,
sincerely, I do.

It is just...
this is the best way

I know how
and sometimes
I know it is not enough.

And I know it hurts,
both ways, too.

You love me
and you show it too much

and I love you
and I show it too little…

but nonetheless,
it doesn't mean you are right

or I am wrong.

It just means
we've both had different paths

and sadly,
the things I've been through

have made it hard
for me to show you.

I hope you understand this.

I hope one day
you can forgive me

for all the things
I should have done.

For all the things
I left unsaid

and for all the untouched pieces
left on the table—

for you to try
to put back together

when you feel most alone.

I'm sorry...
about everything.

I really am.

WRONG THING

Maybe you're focusing
on the wrong things.

Maybe right now,
at this very moment,

the universe isn't guiding you
toward love.

Toward finding someone to hold on to.

There's a time
and a place for everything

and it always comes to you
when you need it most.

So maybe all of this sadness
isn't meant to be yours,

isn't meant to be
held on to

for this long.

Maybe it's something
you're blindly inflicting
on yourself.

Something you know
you want to free yourself from

but can't

because you've invested
so much into it.

Hell,
I know what I'm saying

gets old
and preachy

and maybe even too intense...

but you have to learn
to loosen up your grip a little.

You have to learn
to let go,

and slowly, too—day by day

but only if
it makes the process easier.

Only if
it means putting your health
and your self-worth first—
before anything

or anyone else.

Because your life is about you.

About self-respect,
self-love, and your well-being.

And if someone you deeply love
isn't there for you,

isn't on the same page,
or even understand

what it is you both deserve...

then maybe
it's time to move on.

I'm sorry to be so harsh
and maybe sound a bit selfish...

but you only live once
and your time shouldn't be spent

on anyone who doesn't love themselves.

It shouldn't be spent
on chasing the wrong people

or dwelling on
what terribly hurts.

That's not the way it works.

That's not the way
it should be.

Sadly,
what's meant to be

will be
and what isn't…

you have to learn to say good-bye,
live with it,

and believe
that sometimes

good things do
come with sorrow.

You have to let things run their course
and let go

when you must
and hang on

when you know

there's still something worth
hanging on to.

NO ONE SAYS

No one ever said
loving you was going to be
this hard.

No one ever said
it would be this complicated,

this harsh to deal with.

At first,
I wasn't sure what this was,
what it was going to be.

All I thought was
why not.

I had nothing better to do,
therefore,

I gave whatever interest I had.
I gave whatever little time I had.

I gave it some of my attention,
some of my soul.

And in no time,
I watched it flourish,
and what once was a spark turned

into a torch—into a forest
on fire.

And I watched it flame.
I watched it light

the whole goddamn sky.

And it was beautiful.

It all was.

From the moment it bloomed
to the moment it slipped away.

And I never regretted it.
I never second-guessed it.

Or shot it to hell.

Because it was a good run,
a good time…

a moment caught in a jar of dreams.

But no one ever said
it was going to be easy.

And it wasn't,
that is,
having enough courage

to make it work
and having enough courage
to let it all go.

It's been several years now.

And through the ins
and outs of my life,

someway, somehow,
every once in a while,

you come to mind.

And I can't help but to wonder
what has become of your life.

What became of your heart.

Because you gave me
some of my greatest years, kid,

you really did.

Some unforgettable times.

And now,
like all men who are ill with regret,
all I can do is

sit around

and revisit what we once had.

Revisit how it ended
and see if there was

any other way
around our fallout.

I wonder,
you know,

about everything.

About how different our lives
would be

and if waking up next to you
would have brought me closer

to happiness
or if it would have brought me closer

to my doom.

I wonder, you know...
and that's all I can do.

It's sad.
It really is,

because after all this time,

my mind is still free
and my heart is still trying to figure out

how to live without you.

How to make sense
of all the things

we both chose to ignore
and of all the things

we thought we knew
but clearly didn't.

Life is hard, it truly is…
and so,

I can't help but to wonder why…

it's so hard to say good-bye…
even

after all these years.

Damn.

GOOD WORDS

We all need
some good words to come by

and we all need
someone to lean on.

Someone to pour ourselves into
and talk to.

Someone to inspire us
and remind us

of how it'll all be okay
soon.

Someone who'll help us
battle our demons

and someone
who'll lift us up

when the whole goddamn world
seems to be falling apart.

We all need this sometimes.

We all need…
a friend,

a lover,

someone—anyone,

to protect us
from ourselves.

RUNNING AWAY

You're over there
and I'm running over here.

Oceans apart
but it feels like worlds.

You're over
there living your life

as you should be.

Meeting new people.
Doing new things.

And I'm over here,
faraway,

dreaming about you.

Watching you smile from afar,
smiling back at you

as if
you were getting closer.

As if
we were getting closer.
It makes me feel good inside.

You make me feel good inside.

And although
you're not here,

a part of me still believes

that maybe one day
you will be.

That maybe one day
we'll share the same sky.

The same moon.
The same ocean.

The same coffee shop
and the same room.

I wish all these things for us
because you,

like no one else—make me
feel alive inside.

Make me feel
like I have something

to look forward to.

I like your energy, kid.

I really do.

It takes me to a place
where only the young at heart can reside.

Where only the beautiful can enter.

This,
I rarely say to anyone...

I want your friendship,
your love,
your soul,

and I want to take it
where no one has dared to go before.

I wish I could hold you tightly
and reassure you

of how much I *still* care.

THE THE THE

The violence.
The abuse.

The mistreatment.
The racism.

The hate.
The discrimination.

The inequality.

This is *not* who we are.

This is *not* who we were meant to be.

This is *not* how we were designed—created.

And I can't define
what we are exactly

but I know
it is not those things.

I know
it is not darkness.

It is not the greed,
the power,

and the war of men.

These money driven men.

These false gods.

I've seen the goodness.
I've watched the links of love
connect like chains.

Holding those
who want change

together.

Who want peace and security.

I've seen all of these things
come out of everyone

I've ever met.

The light flowing through their eyes.

The dreams of men.
The dreams of women.

We are all chasing the *same thing*.

We all want to share our lives
with those we love most.

We all want shelter,
clean food, and water.

Good health
and good company

and moments
that'll take our breath away.

We all want respect of our religion
and respect of being ourselves.

I'm sure there are more things
but they cannot come to mind.

We all just want to live comfortably,
without being hated on,

without being pinned down
to the floor like broken tiles.

We want to breathe on our own
without worrying about the cost of air.

So why try to destroy
other people's lives

that do not revolve around yours.

Why try to cage other people
for what they believe in.

Why?

There is no reason to.

I'm sorry to sound too preachy,
they are just some things

I need to get out of my chest.

It's simple.

Treat everyone
how you'd like to be treated yourself.

Everything else is politics
and propaganda

and should be avoided
and or ignored.

FAKE LOVE

I do not want
your fake love.

Your small talk.

Your *make believe*
interest in me.

I don't need any of that.

If you want to talk
to me,
then talk to me.

But please,
be gentle with me.

I'm an artist
and I'm sensitive about my shit.

About what I feel,
speak, and do.

If you want
to get to know me,

then by all means,
let it be with kindness.

Let it be with tenderness.

Let it be real
and full of love.

Lover or not.

Be kind with me.
Be careful with me.

And if you want me,
then let it be known.

I don't have time
for things with no meaning.

For thoughtless,
mindless things.

Give me something real.
Something to lean on,

you know?

That's all we want
in the end.

Someone who can bring out
the best version of ourselves.

Someone who can make

this existence special.

Is that too much to ask for?

Give me your soul
and I'll give you mine in return.

A fair shake
at love.

DESTROY ME NOT

You may try
to destroy me.

You may try
to hurt my feelings

over my race,
over what I say

or do.

You may even
laugh at me

and spread rumors around.

But I'll tell you this,
I am covered with the blood
of my ancestors

and they have bled
and they have bled well

and enough.

And because of them,
I am stronger.

Because of them,
I am still here.

I'm still here

with a back full of wounds,
a heart full of splinters,

and my hands
full of calluses.

I'm kind
because I've had it harder
than you.

I've gone through hell.

I've smiled at the devil
and survived.

So go ahead.
Grab your sword.

Drop your bombs.
Shoot your guns at me
and my people.

You may hurt our reputations.

You may censor our voices
and even kill us...

but know

that there's nothing
we haven't been through.

There's nothing
we haven't overcome.

Today is not promised
but our dreams

and our hopes
will live on

forever.

And eventually,
they will reach your children's children.

And when that day comes...

it will all be beautiful.
Believe that.

GIFT OF GIVING

It's a gift
and a curse,

what I do.

What I write
and how I connect
with people.

I get messages daily.

Some good,
some bad,

and some sad.

It's hurts sometimes
to read what I'm sent.

It really burns my soul.

"I lost my brother to suicide."

*"My father passed 18 years ago.
I never got the chance to meet him."*

*"My boyfriend died 3 weeks ago
and I'm so lost without him."*

"My mother just died
and I'm crying reading your work."

These are the kind of messages
that shatter me.

The kind I don't like reading
because they make me feel

a certain way.

They make me wish
I can heal these people,

comfort them,
make the pain go away.

It hurts
and it does

because I can feel
their pain.

I feel it all through their words.

It's a curse, you know...
to feel everything so deeply,

to really feel things,
so much

that it makes you cry.

So much
that it moves you—it hits you

so hard
that you're left thinking
about it for days.

It's a curse,
indeed it is,

but it is also a gift
because I am able to respond

and connect with them,
share stories with them.

Make them laugh
or cry with them.

Make them feel better
or make them forget,

but only for a little while.

It is a gift
and a curse,

what I do.

It is heaven
and hell.

And sometimes I am flying,
while other times

I am drowning with no one
to guide me toward the shore.

I love you all...

Stay strong,
and in one breath,

please believe when I say:

you are not alone.

REAL TIME

We are influenced greatly
by the things we see.

So much
that we don't have time

to work on ourselves.

Time to really do
what we want to do.

We are blinded
by what we see.

What we read.

It affects us in such a way
that we don't even think

what it is.

No one is prepared
to be themselves

but we are all prepared
to die for things

we don't believe in.

To fight someone else's war,
one we barely understand

for ourselves.

We are all willing
to sacrifice a piece of our identity

at the cost of these brands
and corporations.

Where have we gone?
What has the world done to us?

Why can't I think for myself?

Like the things
I want to like

without being judged.

Say the things
I want to say

without being *hated* on.

Why can't all of us
understand this.

Why can't we respect
one another without letting

the sources influence
the way we should treat

other people.

Why can't we love.
Why can't we help one another.

Be there
for one another.

My sweet people.

We are not free,
although we think we are,

but we are not.

I can't go online
without being told
what to feel.

I can't live my life
without paying some kind of bill.

And I can't do the things
I want

without some kind
of price—sacrifice.

This burdens me.

It blinds me
and I'm trying to see

over the walls.

I'm trying to break free
and I urge this of you,

my sweet people.

Think for yourselves.
Think for yourselves.
Think for yourselves.

Do what's right,
if you feel it in your bones.

Love
who you want
to love,

if you seek it
in your heart.

Believe
in what you must

and don't let
the social extremities

direct your path.

Learn this.
Practice this.

Find your order—your truth
and follow it.

Let your mind
influence your actions

and let your heart
represent your soul.

Do this.
Live by this.

There is no better way
to write your history.

To tell your story.

BE KIND

Be kind to people.

To the strange.
To the broken hearted.

To the ones who have lost all hope.

Be kind to people.

To the lost.
To the empty.

To the ones who know love
and to the ones who do not know love.

Be kind to people.

To everyone you meet
and everyone you do not meet.

To your friends when you are angry
and to those you who let you down when
you need them most.

Be kind, my sweet people, be kind.

I know it is hard to remember.

I know some, but not all, are only kind when
it benefits them or when life is going their
way.

But you have to be kind to people.

Not judge people or assume you know...
when you really do not.

Be kind.

Does it really take too much time?
Does it really affect your ego or hurt your
pride?

Be kind, my sweet people, be kind.

Be madly in love with spreading it. With
becoming it.
With showing it to those who have yet to
practice it.

Be kind.

There is no better way to have people by
your side.
No better way to move them—to inspire
them.
And no better way to make the world a
better place.

WHAT YOU RISK

You risk so much
for a chance to be loved

and without the use
of words,

that says a lot
about who you are.

About what you cherish
and value.

About the kind of future
you'd like to see

for yourself
and others.

You want to cure people's souls.

You want bitterness to vanish
and gentleness
to proceed—to prosper.

You risk so much for love,
too much—almost everything,

but that doesn't hold you back.

That doesn't pull you away
from the real questions.

The real problems.

From sharing something beautiful
with someone who matters.

You risk so much
for a chance to be understood,
too much.

For a chance to overcome

the chaos
and darkness.

For a chance to unlearn
what you've learned,

to reinvent yourself again...

and again...
and again...
and again.

You risk so much
to meet real people.

People who offer
real love

and operate through real feelings—
real solutions, you know?

Real things that save
real people.

You risk so much,
you do,

and you lose so much
while doing so,

but you also gain
something back in return.

You gain experience.
You gain lessons.

You gain this deep
appreciation for life

and people.

This deep sense
of connectivity.

And it is all

for goodness and forgiveness
and strength and perseverance.

All these things
that make this human experience

beautiful.

You risk so much,
too much,

for peace and light...

for the people you know
and for the ones
you have yet to meet.

Keep doing it.

It makes you beautiful
and it encourages me.

It makes me believe
that there are still some good people

out there
worth loving.

Thank you
for what you do.

You have no idea
how important you are.

NOT GOOD EVER

I'm not very good at this,
so I will just get straight to it.

Are you still thinking of him?
Is he still on your mind?

You can tell me the truth, baby.

You don't have to lie.
You don't have to pretend
with me.

Does he still have your heart?

Do you still belong to him
although you know he has moved on?

Are you still hurting inside?
Still hurting over the past?

Still trying to forget?

I know what that's like.
I've been there.

I've had a bad case—maybe
even the worst.

Who knows,
it doesn't matter,

but I know how it is
to be with someone

while having someone else
in your heart.

While having someone else
in your mind.

And it's hard finding balance
between the two.

Between your future
and your past.

Between you who love
and who you want to love.

But you cannot force it.

You cannot want to love me
while loving someone else.

That's not how it works.

The human heart
only has enough room

for one.

Enough space
and enough time, too.

And I know
I'm speculating

and maybe
even looking way too much into it,

but I could tell
you're missing something

or maybe even someone.

I could tell
by the way your eyes light up

when you have
an unread message.

I could tell
by the way you lose your breath

everytime someone you know
mentions his name.

I could tell
and my god,

I want to be wrong...

sincerely, I do,
but you still love him.

You still wonder what your life
could have been

if you were still together.

You're still breaking over it
and then there's me.

And you have me here—collecting
all of your pieces

because I care.

Because I care about YOU, kid,
and your well-being.

I do,
but you cannot tell me

you love me
while being in love with someone else.

You cannot use me
to kill time.

You cannot be with me

only to see
if I could make you forget

about him.

That's not how it works
and that's not fair for anyone...

including yourself.

My sweet girl,
you're in a difficult place
right now,

trapped between two worlds...
and I just want to see

you bloom.

I just want to see you happy...
with whomever

you want,
even if it's not me.

And I'm sorry about this.

I'm sorry I have to go.
But I can't seem to find it in me

to be with you

while you're in love
with someone else,
at least not romantically.

Maybe in another life
things could have been different

and we could have been together
without any interruptions

at all...

until we meet again.

GO WITH IT

Go with it.

It is only mental.
Emotional.

These attachments.

These things
you don't want

to let go of.

These things
you don't want

to adapt to.

Go with it.

You're a survivor.

The change of time.
The change of thought

and the change
of ones heart.

Go with it.

If you feel it.
Take a leap of faith.

Move to that city
you've always dreamed of.

Tell that one person
how you feel.

How you see your life
with them.

Go with it.

Live with it.
I know it is a shot
in the dark

but you must take it.

Go for it
without regret.

Without shame—without fear.

Go with it
and I mean
all of it with bravery.

With style.
With contradiction.

With your humanity.

There is no space here
for doubt.

There is no space here
for insecurity.

Go with it.
Go through it.

What you desire
is just a few feet

from your grasp.

Whether it be a new job.
A new interest.

A new love.
A new house.

A new goal.
A new life.

Anything... go with it—
with dedication.

With heart.
With sweat and with blood.

Go with it.

Do it.
Do it.
Do it.

You are meant to do
so much more.

You're meant to chase…

To feel.
To dream.
To worship.
To heal.
To grow.
To hold…

everything you want
with love, forever…

as long as you
go with it, forever.

Require it, forever,
and never give up

on yourself, forever.

Keep pushing.
Keep living.

Keep searching
for the light

in the darkest of places.

Keep finding the inspiration.
Keep preaching goodness

and spreading love
and go on with it…

go far with it…
if it's the last thing you do.

And don't have it any
other way…

go on with it…

forever.

BALANCE

Find your balance.

Don't let your heart
turn on you.

Don't let your thoughts
go against what you feel.

I've met good people
who've done bad things.

Good people
who've made mistakes.

Find that thing,
that voice within you.

Within your gut.

That feeling.
That one moment
that speaks to you—that tells you

it's okay
to not be

the most prepared.

That tells you
it's okay to have things

fall apart on you.

That it's okay to try—to give it
your all gloriously and fail.

Find your balance.
Your truth.

Your voice
even at your worst.

You are not unworthy
of good things.

You're not unworthy
of love.

Of vanity.
Of self-admiration.

You owe it to yourself
to be proud.

You owe it to yourself
to know what you deserve.

To know
who you are

without the social commentaries
pressing on against you—leaning
on you—blinding you

from the truth.

You owe it to yourself
to be real

and to find someone
who could be real with you.

Find your balance.
Find your peace.

Find the fight in you
and stand against

whatever it is
that brings you down.

Whatever it is
that hurts.

Find the love in you
and hold on to it.

And never lose sight of it.

Never let it betray you.
Find your balance,

find it,
and never let it go.

I promise you,

it will not
bring you down.

It will give you
balance.

Especially

when and where you need it most.

TO FORGET

I get a message from a girl and she says,

"You're my god."

in the end of her message.

now this terrifies me.
The fact that some of my readers actually
feel this way. It's not the first time I've read
this and it probably won't be the last.

But please, dear reader,
I'm not your god. I'm not a god. I barely
know how to live. I barely know what to do.
I'm just beginning to figure out who I am—
how to express myself, you know?

So please, dear readers, don't ever say that to
me or to anyone living in this forsaken earth.
It's blasphemous.

I am no one god. No one is. We're all just
ordinary people looking for salvation in
people. Looking for truth and looking for
others like us… who can relate with what
we've been through.

So let us praise the God's,

the real God's,

and ask them for forgiveness
and guidance

in all the things we do.